SQL

The Topnotch Crash Course of 2016 and Learn 1 Day for Beginner's plus advance Training (SQL, SQL Course, SQL Development, SQL Books)

By:
James Stevens

Table of Contents

Introduction 3

Chapter 1: SQL Basics 4

Chapter 2: SQL Syntax 8

Chapter 3: Creating a Database in SQL Server 19

Chapter 4: SQL Tables 24

Chapter 5: Handling Data in SQL 31

Chapter 6: Primary and Foreign Keys 33

Conclusion 37

Introduction

With the increasing use of computers everywhere in the lives of people today, creation and gathering of so much data is slowly become the order or the day. This is rampant in the business industry but it is also seen in other areas, even for people who use their computers for personal reasons. Good thing about data creation is that you get to use the same data later on, as many times as you want, without the need to create more data. That is why creation of databases is important.

In a business setting for instance, a lot of data is generated every day and the same data is required for the day to day operations of the business for so many years. Creating a database for that data ensures that the data is safe, and it can be retrieved easily for use at a later date. This is the reason why mastery of programing languages is necessary because it helps in the creation of these databases and retrieval of that data, interpretation and manipulation very easy for everyone else.

SQL is an important programming language as it makes database creation and management of the data in a database very easy. It is a language that will benefit any type of person especially those who intend to work in a business environment because this will make working much easier for them. It also increases your chances of scoring a good employment these days, since this is a very important skills for many employers today.

Chapter 1: SQL Basics

SQL is an ordinary programming language that is used for creating and accessing databases. A lot of businesses are gathering so much data everyday but the challenge comes when many people are required to access and use that data in their day to day operations. Being able to access data and to save data in a database makes working in a modern business very easy that is why mastering SQL is an important thing for any person that is working in a business setting today. SQL will give anyone an upper hand in understanding how databases work and how they can create their own databases for easier saving and manipulation of data.

SQL is a very popular programming language mainly because it runs in so many platforms, for instance in Windows, Linux, MacOSX, open Saris among so many others.

SQL, also structured Query Language is a programming language that is used for special purposes. It is used to manage data that is stored in a relational database management system and also for processing data in streams in an interactive data stream management system. It was originally based on tuple relational calculus and relational algebra.

With SQL, you get data definition language, data manipulating language as well as data control language. It covers inserting data, queries, updating and selecting data, schema creation and also modification as well as data access control. Many people refer to it as a declarative language but it has some procedural element.

SQL language Elements

SQL programming language is divided into different language element which include:

a) Clauses- these are the constituent mechanisms of queries and statements. In most cases, clauses are optional.

b) Expressions- these are the ones that are able to bring forth either tables or scalar values that consist of rows and columns of data in SQL

c) Predicates-these are the ones which specify which conditions should be evaluated to the three-valued in SQL, which are true, false and unknown. They also specify conditions which can be used to evaluate the Boolean truth values. The predicates are meant to restrict the properties of queries and statements, or to alter the flow of the program.

d) The Queries- these are the elements which recover the data that is based on an exact criteria. They are very important element in SQL.

e) Statements- these are elements which could have an insistent effect on schemes and data. They may also have control over transactions, the flow of the program, the connections, the sessions, or the diagnostics. The statement elements in SQL also include a semicolon statement terminator. Statements may not be vital on each platform but they are considered as very important elements in QL grammar.

f) The unimportant whitespace is also a significant element in SQL but it is overlooked in SQL queries and statements. This way it becomes very easy to set-up SQL codes for easier readability.

SQL operators

There are several SQL operators you should start learning:

- o = meaning equal to
- o < > meaning not equal to
  - ➢ meaning greater than
- o < Meaning less than
- o >= meaning greater than or equal to
- o <= meaning less than or equal to
- o BETEEN meaning in between an inclusive range
- o LIKE used to match a character pattern
- o IN which means equal to one of numerous possible values
- o IS or IS NOT meaning compare to null (null in this case is a missing data)
- o IS NOT DISTINCT FROM meaning that it is equal to the value or both of them are nulls
- o AS will be used to change the field name when you are viewing results.

These are the common operators that you will find while using SQL. There are other operators that are used from time to time, only that they are not as popular for instance:

- o The skyline operator which is used for finding only those records that are not 'worse' than all the others.

SQL Queries

A query is the most used operation in SQL. It makes use of the SELECT statement which is declarative. SELECT is the one that retrieves data from one or more tables and expressions. With queries, you will be able to describe any data that you desire, when you can leave out the data management system to carry out the planning, enhancing and performing any physical operations that may be necessary in order to produce the result that is desirable.

A query comes with a list of columns which it includes in the final result.

Chapter 2:
SQL Syntax

SQL syntax is the best way to start for anyone that wants to use SQL in creating their databases. There are so many SQL commands and each of them has its own syntax. Understanding this syntax will make learning SQL very easy since you can always refer to the syntax in order to understand what needs to be done at each step of the way. It is also the only faster way one can learn SQL.

1. Select statement

This means selecting column name from the table name or selecting data from the table that is in a database. A table in this case is like a container in the database where information is stored. The select statement is represented as:

SELECT "column_name" FROM "table_name";

There are different ways through which you can recover data from a table

- recovering a column
- recovering multiple columns
- retrieving all columns

We can use the table below for clear illustration of the above three cases:

Table *Sales_Information*

Stock_Name	Sales	Txn_Date
Atlanta	1500	Jan-05-1989
San Francisco	250	Jan-07-1989
Washington DC	300	Jan-08-1989
Ohio	700	Jan-08-1989

In order to retrieve data from a single column, you have to specify the column between SELECT and FROM, from which the data is being retrieved. Here is an example of a command you can use:

SELECT Stock_Name FROM sales_Information;

To select more than one column, you specify the columns from which the data is to be retrieved. Here is an example of a SQL command that you can use:

SELECT Stock_Name, Sales FROM Sales_Information;

On the other hand, you can use either of the following ways in order to select all columns from a table.

- you can list down all the columns from where the data is being retrieved
- You can use asterisks symbol. this is the easiest way out
-

Here is an example of a command you can use for this:

*SELECT * FROM sales_Information;*

2. Distinct

With the above keyword, you are able to take all information from a column or from multiple columns on a table. What happens when you want to select a separate element from a given table? This is when Distinct is applied in SQL. What you do is to simply add **Distinct** after **Select**. Here is the syntax for this:

SELECT DISTINCT "column_name"
FROM "table_name";

In the above example, in order to select all distinct stocks in the Sales_Information table, this is the code that you key in:
SELECT DISTINCT Stock_Name FROM Sales_Information;

3. Where

The Where clause will be used to filter the results that are based on certain conditions. This means that it is the clause to use when you want to conditionally select data from a given table. Here is the syntax that will be using **Where** in a select statement:

SELECT "column_name"
FROM "table_name"
WHERE "condition";

A condition in this case can comprise of a single comparison clause, which is what is referred to as a simple condition, or many comparison clauses that have been put together using OR or AND operators, also called compound conditions.

In the table we used earlier:

Table **Sales_Information**

Stock_Name	Sales	Txn_Date
Atlanta	1500	Jan-05-1989
San Francisco	250	Jan-07-1989
Washington DC	300	Jan-08-1989
Ohio	700	Jan-08-1989

In order to select all the sales that were above $1,000, you use the code:

SELECT Store_Name
FROM Store_Information
WHERE Sales > 1000;

And the results you get will be

Stock_Name
Atlanta

The use of **Where clause with OR operator**-if you want to view information from the table above, with data sales below 500 or with transaction dates Jan-07-1999, you use this SQL command:

SELECT *
FROM Stock_Information
WHERE Sales < 500 OR Txn_Date = 'Jan-07-1999';

Use of **Where Clause with Update or Delete**- together with Select Statement, the Where clause can be used together with Update and Delete statements

4. And/Or

The compound conditions that we mentioned in the Where clause section are comprised of multiple simple conditions that are connected by AND or OR. In SQL, there is no limit as to the number of simple conditions that you can present in a single statement. Here is the syntax that you can use for the compound statements:

SELECT "column_name"
FROM "table_name"
WHERE "simple condition"
{ [AND|OR] "simple condition"}+;

Where the use of { }+ is an indication that the expression that is inside the brackets will occurs one or several times. And/Or indicates that you can use either AND or OR. This ( ) sign can also be used in order to show the order of the condition.

5. In

In keyword is used twice in SQL and here, we will cover the use that is related to Where clause. When it is used in this case, you should be able to know the value of the returned values that you want to see for at least one of the columns because it limits the selection criteria to one or more discrete values. This is the syntax that you use when using **In**:

SELECT "column_name"
FROM "table_name"
WHERE "column_name" IN ('value1', 'value2', ...);

In the parenthesis, the number of values can be one or more and every value that you use should be separated by a comma. Numerals or characters can be used in this case as values. In this case, if there is only one value inside the parenthesis, this command will be the same as:

WHERE "column_name" = 'value1'

6. Between

The between operator in SQL is the one used to select a range. The syntax you will use for **Between** operator is:

SELECT "column_name"
FROM "table_name"
WHERE "column_name" BETWEEN 'value1' AND 'value2';

With this syntax, you will get all the rows whose columns have a value that is between value1 and value2.

Between is an inclusive operator and this means that value1 and value2 will be included in the result that you will get. If you want to exclude value1 and value2 but you want to capture everything in between, you will have to change the query. Try this it:

SELECT "column_name"
FROM "table_name"
WHERE ("column_name" > 'value1')
AND ("column_name" < 'value2');

Between operator can also be used to exclude a range of values and this is done by adding Not before between. Here is an example of a command:

SELECT *
FROM Stock_Information
WHERE Sales NOT BETWEEN 280 and 1000;

7. Like

LIKE is another keyword that is used together with the WHERE clause. Instead of specifying exactly what is desired as in the case with IN or spelling out a range like it is done with BETWEEN, LIKE will allow you to do a search that is based on a pattern. Here is its syntax:

SELECT "column_name"
FROM "table_name"
WHERE "column_name" LIKE {PATTERN};

Pattern in this case consists of wild cards. Using the example above:

Table *Sales_Information*

Stock_Name	Sales	Txn_Date
Atlanta	1500	Jan-05-1989
San Francisco	250	Jan-07-1989
Washington DC	300	Jan-08-1989
Ohio	700	Jan-08-1989

You can use this syntax

SELECT *
FROM Store_Information
WHERE Store_Name LIKE '%AT%';

14

In order to find all stock whose names have AT and the results will be like:

Store_Name	**Sales Txn_Date**
Atlanta	*1500 Jan-05-1989*

8. Order By

Select and Where are used to retrieve data from a table but sometimes you will be required to put down the output in a special order, either ascending, descending, following a certain text value or numerical value. In this case, you will use **Order By.** This is the syntax for this statement:

SELECT "column_name"
FROM "table_name"
[WHERE "condition"]
ORDER BY "column_name" [ASC, DESC];

The use of [ ] here means that Where statement can be used here, it is optional. In case it is used, it should come ahead of the ORDER By clause. Use of ASC on the other hand shows that the results you will get will appear in an ascending order. DESC will mean the outcome will be presented in a descending order. However, if you have not used ASC or DESC, the default choice is taken, which is ASC.

You can Order By over one column and in that case, the clause above will change to:

ORDER BY "column_name1" [ASC, DESC], "column_name2"
[ASC, DESC]

If you chose ascending order for the two columns then the result will be ordered as per the first column. However, if there is a relation in the first column, the output will assume the ascending order as per the 2nd column.

Other than sorting according to the name of the column, you can sort as per the column position that you will have to specify on your SQL query. So as to show the column that you want to apply the ORDER BY statement. With that, the first column will be 1, the second one 2, the third one 3 and so on. Here is an example:

SELECT Stock_Name, Sales, Txn_Date
FROM Stock_Information
ORDER BY 2 DESC;

Note that the columns that you will use to categorize the result will not appear in the SELECT clause.

You can also sort the outcome by an expression.

9. Group By

Using the table example above, perhaps you want to calculate the total sales of each stock; you will first of all select the stock name and ten the sales. The other thing you will do is to group the sales figures with the stocks. This is where Group By clause is used and the syntax is as follows:

SELECT "column_name1", SUM("column_name2")
FROM "table_name"
GROUP BY "column_name1";

In the above syntax, you will be able to group by just one column. Supposing you want to group by multiple columns? It is easy to use Group By in more than one columns. The general syntax in this case will be:

SELECT "column_name1", "column_name2", ... "column_nameN", Function("column_nameN+1")
FROM "table_name"
GROUP BY "column_name1", "column_name2", ... "column_nameN";

You can also group by Month/date or week- with this kind of query, you will have to accompany it with Order By keyword in order to have a result that shows time series. Here is an example of a query that you can make in this case:

SELECT Txn_Date, SUM(Sales)
FROM Stock_Information
GROUP BY Txn_Date;

10. Count

This is an arithmetic function that allows you to count the number of rows in a certain SQL table. The syntax that is used here is:

SELECT COUNT("column_name")
FROM "table_name";

If for instance you want to find out the number of stock entries in the table we used above, you use the statement below:

SELECT COUNT (Stock_Name)
FROM Stock_Information;

And the results will be:

COUNT (Store_Name)
4
COUNT can be used together with DISTICT in a statement in order to retrieve the number of separate entries in a table.

11. Having

The HAVING clause is usually reserved for aggregate functions. It will be useful when you want to retrieve data but you want to limit the output to only those which have a corresponding sum. This clause is usually placed at the end of the SQL statement and it can either be used with Group By clause or not. The syntax you will use for having is as follows:
SELECT ["column_name1"], Function("column_name2")

FROM "table_name"
[GROUP BY "column_name1"]
HAVING (arithmetic function condition);

Note that you can select a zero, one or more columns together with the aggregate function. If you select a zero column, you will not need to use the Group By clause.

Chapter 3:
Creating a Database in SQL Server

Like I mentioned above, SQL databases are among the most used databases across the world. This is because of a number of reasons, for instance it is very easy to create. What you need is a graphical user interface program that comes freely like a SQL Server Management. With that in place, creating a database is easy and you can start entering your data in no time at all. Here is how:

1. Start by installing the software(SQL Server Management Studio) to your computer

This is software that is freely available for Microsoft. It will allow you to gain access to and also to work with your SQL server from a graphical interface other than using a command line for the same. The software will also allow you to gain access to a remote request of an SQL server. If not this one, you will require a similar software.

There are other interfaces that are available for other platforms like Mac for instance SQuirreL SQL. Such interfaces may differ but they all work the same.

You can also create a database using the tools available in command line.

2. Once the software has been installed, start it up.

After the installation, you can now start your program. You will be required to choose if you want to connect to a certain server. If there is a server already that is already set and working and you have all the permissions connect access it, just enter its address and the authentication information. But if you want to build your own local database, you will create the Database name and the type of authentication under the **Windows Authentication**.

3. Now locate your database folder

After a connection has been made to the server, whether it is a local connection or a remote one, the Object Explorer will now open on the left hand side of your screen. Right at the top part of your Object Explorer diagram, you will see the server that you are using to. If it has not been expanded, click on the "+" icon that is following it and it will expand.

4. You can now create a fresh database

Spot the database folder and right click on it. Click on New database option from the list that will come up. This will give you a new window which will allow you to organize your database before you start creating it. First of all, you need to give your database a new and unique name, which will make it easy for you to identify it. The other settings can be left just the way they are at default settings unless there is an important change that you want to make. When you give your database a name, there are two other additional files that will be formed automatically, which are log and data files. The data file will be the one that will host all your information in your database and the log file will be the one that will track all the changes that you will make on the database. When satisfied, you can hit OK in order to create your database. Your newly created database will now appear in the extended database Folder, with a cylindrical icon, it will be easy to spot it.

5. Start creating your table

You have to come up with a structure where you will start storing your data and this will be your table. With a table, you can hold all manner of information and data that you want stored in the database. This is an important part before you can go on. To do this, you enlarge the new database that is in your database folder and then right click on the table's icon to select a New Table option. Windows thereafter opens everything else on your screen to let you to work on your new table as much as you want.

6. It's time for the primary key

Primary keys are very important, therefore it is important to let them be the first entry on the first column of your SQL table. They act as the ID number or the highest number that helps you quickly remember what you have put in record in that table. In order to create your primary keys, enter ID on the field that has the Column Name and enter INT into the field marked Data Type. As of the Allow Nulls, ensure that they are all unchecked. Now hit the key icon in your toolbar in order to make this column your primary key. With this, you will not have null values but if you want to have a null value as your principal entry, you will check to Allow Nulls.

Scroll down the column properties to find the option Identity Specification. Expanding this option and setting it to a YES will ensure that the values on the ID column increases automatically on every entry that you will make. With this, all your new entries will be effectively numbered in the right order.

7. It's time to understand how tables are designed

This is an important part so as to find it easy to enter information in your database. With tables, you will get different columns or fields and every column denotes an aspect of every database entry that you will make. If you have a database for people in an organization for instance, your will have a FirsName column entry, LastName column entry, Address, Phone Number and such like entries.

8. The other columns

When all the fields of the Primary Key have been filled in, other fields will automatically form beneath it. These will be the fields where all your other data will be entered. You are now free to enter data in those fields the way you want to. The right data type has to be chosen though so that it will match the data that you have filled in that column.

nchar(#) represents the type of data that should be used for the text for instance addresses, names among others. In the parenthesis will be a number which is the highest number that will be allowed in that field. You can set the limit in order to allow the size of your database to remain manageable. You can for instance use this format for the phone numbers in order to make it hard for you to perform mathematical function on the numbers.

int on the other hand represents data in whole numbers. This is the one that is used in the field marked ID.

decimal(x,y) will save your numbers in a decimal format. The number within the parenthesis will signify the total number of numerals and the other number of digits that will follow the decimals respectively.

9. When all that is done, save the table

First save the table then you can start entering information on your columns. To do this, click on the Save button on your toolbar, then enter the name for your table. It is important to have a unique and easy to understand name for your table so that you will be able to tell what the table is all about without going through the data in it. This will be very useful especially once you start using large databases that have so many tables.

Chapter 4:
SQL Tables

An interactive database system will have one or more objects. These are what we call tables. Data or information for the databases are stored in these tables. Tables are identified with their names, which should be unique. They also contain columns and rows. Under columns, you will have the column name, the data type and any other attribute that you will want to have on your column. In the rows, you will have records of data that is contained in the columns. Every row will have one piece of data. Here is an example of a SQL table:

Weather			
city	**state**	**high**	**low**
Phoenix	Arizona	109	92
Tucson	Arizona	115	99
Flagstaff	Arizona	90	71
San Diego	California	79	58
Albuquerque	New Mexico	78	73

Since you do not know beforehand what your data storage needs will be like, you will have to create tables that will meet your needs in your database. For this, you will have to use the CREATE TABLE statement. This is one of the most important mechanisms of SQL. The SQL syntax that is used in the creation of table sis:

CREATE TABLE "table_name"
("column 1" "data type for column 1" [column 1 constraint(s)],
"column 2" "data type for column 2" [column 2 constraint(s)],
...
[table constraint(s)]);

In the above syntax, Column 1 and Column 2 are the names of each column. After the name of the column, you specify the data type that you will enter in that column. A typical data type will be represented in integers for instance 1, 2, 3, in real numbers for instance in 1.46, 9.82, in strings for instance sql, in data/time expressions for instance '2002-JAN-24 03:22:22 and also in binary form. Databases will differ in the kind of data type that you can enter, therefore it is important to consult with your data specific reference first so as to know the type of data that you can enter.

The [ ] symbol is used to mean that the phrase that is inside it may ensue zero times, one, two or more times. You can or cannot specify the column and table restrictions. Your column or table may also have more than one restriction.

Here are some of the restrictions that can be used when one is creating a SQL table:

- NOT NULL Constraint- this restriction will ensure that a column cannot have a NULL value.

- DEFAULT Constraint: this restriction will provide a default value for a column when no value has been specified.

- UNIQUE Constraint: this restriction ensures that all values in a column are different from each other.

25

- CHECK Constraint: this restriction will make sure that all the values in a column are satisfying a certain criteria.

- Primary Key Constraint: this restriction is used to identify a row in the table uniquely.

- Foreign Key Constraint: this restriction is used to ensure referential truthfulness of the data.

Here is an example:

CREATE TABLE Employees
(First_Name char(50),
Last_Name char(55),
Address char(55),
City char(55),
Country char(30),
Birth_Date datetime);

Above is a syntax that can be used to record customer information with First Name, Last Name, Address, City, Count and Birth Date information on the columns. Here, there was no use of any constraints. What would happen if you want to add a few constraints, say a constraint that want to use a different country as the default country, say UK? In this case, the SQL statement will be;

CREATE TABLE Customer
(First_Name char(50),
Last_Name char(50),
Address char(50),
City char(50),
Country char(25) default 'United States',
Birth_Date datetime);

Sometimes you realize that the table structure that you need is the same as another table that is already in the database. If that is the case, you do not need to type in all the column names and data types as well as the constraints details. What you do is to use CREATE TABLE in order to make a copy of the table structure. Here is the syntax you can use to achieve this:

CREATE TABLE "table_name" AS
[SQL Statement];
If you want to copy both the structure and the data of Table 1 into Table 2, you will use this statement:
CREATE TABLE Table2 AS
SELECT * FROM Table1;

If on the other and you are interested in only the structure of able 1 and not the data, you can use this QL statement:

CREATE TABLE Table2 AS
SELECT * FROM Table1
WHERE 0 = 1;

When **WHERE 0 = 1** clause is used, it means that it is false that is why you will not be able to copy any data from Table 1 to table 2 but just the structure.

Inserting data to a table

The **insert statement** will be the one to use in order to integrate or to add a row of information into the table. If for instance you want to enter some archives into a table, you write the keywords INSERT then you follow it with the name of the table, then then an opening parenthesis, then keyword values, then the information in a list, then the closing parenthesis. The data that you will enter in this case will appear in the rows. They have to match with the names of the columns which you have specified. Strings must be bounded in single quotes but numbers should not be bound. Here is an illustration of this:

insert into "tabletitle"
(first_column,...last_column)
Data (first_data,...last_data);

With this example, the name of the first column will correspond with the value *James* and the column name *Country* will correspond to the value name *USA*.
insert into voters

(first, last, age, address, city, state, country)
values (James, John, 50, '1120 West Virginia,
James Associates, USA);

Like in the example, all strings should be enclosed in a single quote.

Drop Table

The need to get rid of a table in a databases may arise and when it happens, it should not be a problem at all. It should in fact be done immediately to avoid facing maintenance issues later on. Good thing is that SQL allows one to do it with ease, sing the DROP TABLE command. Here is its syntax:

DROP TABLE "table_name";

You can DROP a single TABLE or multiple TABLES at the same time. The above statement a be used to DROP just one table but if you want to drop more than one table at a time, you will have to come up with list of all the tables that you wish to drop, separating each of them by comma after the DROP TBLE clause. Here is an example of a statement that can be used:

DROP TABLE User_Details, Job_List;

Note that if you try to drop a table that does not exists, you will get an error. To prevent getting an error result, there are databases like Oracle and MySQL which allows use of IF EXISTS statement before DROP TABLE command and the name of the table. This will guide the database to perform the DROP TABLE statement only if the table that is to be dropped exists. If the table does not exist, nothing will be executed and you will not get an error message. Here is an example of a DROP TBLE IF EXISTS statement:

DROP TABLE IF EXISTS Sales;

Truncate Table

What happens if you want to get rid of all the data in a table but you do not want to drop that table? For this, you use the Truncate Table Statement. Its syntax is as follows:

TRUNCATE TABLE "table_name";

TRUNCATE TABL and DELETE are two SQL statements that are the same. The only difference is in the amount of system resources that is required during the execution. This will affect the amount of time that it will take to complete the execution. TRUNCATE in this case is faster because it does not record the changes that occur one row at a time but DELETE has to record all the changes, one row at a time.

Chapter 5:
Handling Data in SQL

With an already set table, what is left is to start adding data and saving it to your database. Open your table and then right click on it. Select the edit option. You will have all your fields for you to start entering data. You do not have to fill in the ID field because tis field is filled in automatically. Concentrate on the other fields, making sure that you fill in the right data as per the column name. Go on until all the data that you have at hand has been filled out then you can save the data by executing the table. To do this, click the **EXCUTE** button on your SQL toolbar once you have keyed in all the data that you want to save. The server will start working in the background, analyzing all the data in the columns that you have created.

In case there were errors while you were entering data, they will be shown to you to be able to know which of the fields were filled in incorrectly for you to make the necessary changes. This has to be done before the server finished executing the table. This marks the end of your database cretin, from where you can query the data as much as you want.

Querying data is done for reports or any other administrative reasons. You can also add to the data that you have already saved and also remove any data that you want from your database as I will explain later on.

In order to update or change records that match a specified criteria in SQL, you use the **UPDATE** statement. To achieve this, you will carefully construct a WHERE Clause as illustrated below:

update "tabletitle"
set "columntitle" =
*   "newvalue"*
[,"nextcolumn" =
*   "2newvalue"...]*
where "columntitle"
* OPERATOR "value"*
[and|or "column"
* OPERATOR "value"];*
where [] = optional

In order to deleting records or rows from a table, you will use the **DELETE** Statement using this syntax:

delete from "tabletitle"

where "columntitle"
* OPERATOR "value"*
[and|or "column"
* OPERATOR "value"];*
where [ ] = optional

Chapter 6:
Primary and Foreign Keys

The primary keys and the foreign keys are two kinds of constraints or restrictions that are used in order to apply data reliability in SQL server tables. They are very important objects in a database and they will help you get exactly what you want to achieve with your database.

The primary key constraints

Your SQL table will have a column or a set of columns that contains values which identify every row in that table differently. That column/columns use the primary key of that table and it is the one that enforce the object integrity in the entire table. The primary keys are the ones that guarantee that you will have a unique data all through and they are often defined at the identity column.

Once you give your table a primary key, the database will automatically give your data exceptionality by creating a sole index for the columns with the primary key. If on the other hand you define a primary key on columns exceeding one, your values may be repeated in that column but every blend of values for all those columns in the primary key restraint definition must be different and unique.

Here is an illustration:

merchandiseID	DealerID	Time	Standard Price	Actual Cost
2	2	16	46.90	48.20
3	120	15	34.66	34.89
8	3	17	56.38	59.00
500	8	16	29.80	33.45
570	99	17	45.78	46.78

With this illustration, the merchandkiseID and the dealerID columns are the primary key constraints for the entre table. This is what has ensures that each row in the table has an exclusive blend of the data in the two columns. This way, it will be impossible to duplicate information in rows.

From the table, it is clear that:

- one table can only have one primary key restraint

- A primary key should not go beyond 16 columns as well as an entire key length of nine hundred bytes.

- The index that has been produced by the primary key constraint can't make the index numbers on the table to go beyond 999 ungrouped indexes and one grouped index.

- If you will not specify whether the indexes are clustered or not clustered for your primary constraints, the clustered indexes will be the one that will be used more so if there is no grouped index on that table.

- All the columns that will be defined within the primary key constraint should not defined as null. You have to set their nullability to a number and not null so that you will not have a null value even when you will not specify that in the columns.

- If your primary key has been well-defined on a CLR type of data that is user-defined, its application must support the binary ordering.

The foreign key constraints

A foreign key on the other hand is a column or a set of columns which is useful for starting and imposing a connection between data that has been entered in two SQL tables in order to regulate the data that can be saved in the table with the foreign key. Where the foreign key has been referred to, there is a connection that is created among the two tables once the column/columns which have the primary key value of the table are denoted by the column/ columns in an extra table. This column is the one that converts to a foreign key in the extra table.

A single table can refer to up to 253 other tables as well as columns and make them foreign keys, also the outgoing references.

When working with foreign key constraints:

- Foreign key orientations that go beyond 253 will only be supported for DELET DML operations. MERGE and UPDATE operations are not sustained.

- Any table that has foreign key references to itself will still face the limitation to 253 foreign key orientations.

- Those foreign key references that are greater than 253 are not available for column store keys at the moment, for stretch database, for tables that are memory optimized and also for foreign key tables that are partitioned.

Conclusion

SQL is a different type of programing language. With it, you will be able to create a database and also manage any data that is stored in an interactive database administration system. It is a very easy to master programming language that will make working with databases easier than you previously thought. It is a programming language that is slowly gaining popularity because of its usefulness and also how easy it is and also its relevance in different types of industries today.

Leaning SQL is very easy therefore you can master everything that you need to know in order to start creating your own databases in a day. There are just a few syntax that you need to learn and then you will be creating your tables and saving so much data in no time at all. The advantage you get with SQL is that it has so many features that will enable you to manipulate your data as much as you want and to make it relevant to anyone that will be interested in it.

With this guide, you should be able to start leaning SQL on the right footing. The guide will help you learn the basics of creating tables for instance and how to enter data and manipulate it in your SQL tables. However, you have to know that a lot of time, practice and dedication will be needed for you to become an expert SQL user. You may learn so much in a day but putting it in practice will enable you to start creating and managing your own databases like an expert.

www.ingramcontent.com/pod-product-compliance
Lightning Source LLC
Chambersburg PA
CBHW060935050326
40689CB00013B/3096